AF269740

ALL-STAR SMACK DOWN

ROMAN REIGNS VS. HULK HOGAN

WHO WOULD WIN?

JOSH ANDERSON

Lerner Publications ◆ Minneapolis

Lerner Publications Company
An imprint of Lerner Publishing Group, Inc.
241 First Avenue North
Minneapolis, MN 55401 USA

For reading levels and more information, look up this title at www.lernerbooks.com.

Main body text set in Aptifer Sans LT Pro.
Typeface provided by Linotype AG.

Library of Congress Cataloging-in-Publication Data

Names: Anderson, Josh, author.
Title: Roman Reigns vs. Hulk Hogan : who would win? / Josh Anderson.
Other titles: Roman Reigns versus Hulk Hogan
Description: Minneapolis, MN : Lerner Publications, [2024] | Series: All-star smackdown (Lerner sports) | Includes bibliographical references and index. | Audience: Ages 7–11 | Audience: Grades 4–6 | Summary: "From bulging muscles to adoring fans, pro wrestling superstars Roman Reigns and Hulk Hogan have a lot in common. But only one can be king of the ring. Compare their careers and choose your champion"— Provided by publisher.
Identifiers: LCCN 2023013890 (print) | LCCN 2023013891 (ebook) | ISBN 9798765610275 (library binding) | ISBN 9798765623558 (paperback) | ISBN 9798765614105 (epub)
Subjects: LCSH: Wrestling—Juvenile literature. | Anoa'i, Leati Joseph, 1985—-Juvenile literature. | Hogan, Hulk, 1953—-Juvenile literature. | Wrestlers—Juvenile literature. | Wrestling matches—Juvenile literature. | BISAC: JUVENILE NONFICTION / Sports & Recreation / Wrestling | JUVENILE NONFICTION / Biography & Autobiography / Sports & Recreation
Classification: LCC GV1195.3 .A53 2024 (print) | LCC GV1195.3 (ebook) | DDC 796.812—dc23/eng/20230331

LC record available at https://lccn.loc.gov/2023013890
LC ebook record available at https://lccn.loc.gov/2023013891

Manufactured in the United States of America
4-1012326-51700-2/24/2025

TABLE OF CONTENTS

Introduction
Wrestling Legends 4

Chapter 1
Journey to the Wrestling Ring . . . 8

Chapter 2
Great Moments 14

Chapter 3
Champions 20

Chapter 4
And the Winner Is 24

Smackdown Breakdown 28
Glossary 30
Learn More 31
Index 32

Hulk Hogan

INTRODUCTION

WRESTLING LEGENDS

WrestleMania III took place on March 29, 1987. Nearly 80,000 wrestling fans were at the Silverdome in Pontiac, Michigan, to watch. It was one of the largest crowds in pro wrestling history. In the main event, Hulk Hogan defended his World Wrestling

 **FAST FACTS** 

- ✪ Hulk Hogan held the World Wrestling Entertainment [WWE] Championship belt six times.

- ✪ Hogan won the Royal Rumble twice.

- ✪ Roman Reigns won the WWE title for the fourth time on April 3, 2022.

- ✪ Reigns has held five different championships in the WWE.

Federation (WWF) championship against his old friend Andre the Giant. The Giant hadn't been defeated in many years. He wanted to win Hogan's title.

Early in the match, Hogan tried to body-slam the Giant. But Hogan couldn't lift his 500-pound (227 kg) opponent. Hogan was almost out of energy. He would need to dig deep if he wanted to keep his championship.

Hogan ducked under a clothesline and hit the Giant, knocking him to the ground. The move sent Hogan into Hulk Mode. The burst of energy from Hulk Mode had led him to victory many times before.

Hogan (front) *and Andre the Giant* (back).

Moments later, Hogan tried to body-slam the Giant again. This time, he lifted the Giant successfully! Hogan ended the match with his signature move, the leg drop, and kept his title.

Thirty-five years later, another great champion defended his title at SummerSlam 2022. Roman Reigns fought in a Last Man Standing match. A wrestler loses a Last Man Standing contest when they are unable to stand up for a referee's entire count to ten. Reigns battled Brock Lesnar. They had fought many times before. This would be their last fight.

Lesnar rode a tractor to the ring. He used it to toss Reigns into the ring and to lift half of the ring into the air. After more than 22 minutes of tough fighting, Reigns knocked Lesnar to the ground outside the ring. He covered Lesnar with objects from around the ring, including steel chairs and pieces of the broken announcers table. Reigns climbed on top of the pile, and the referee declared him the winner of the Last Man Standing match.

Reigns and Hogan are two of the most successful pro wrestlers of all time. But which one was the best? Let the smackdown begin!

Roman Reigns (top) pins Brock Lesnar at WWE's 2021 Crown Jewel event.

onstage. They thought he might make a good pro wrestler.

In 1979, Bollea began using the name Hulk Hogan in the ring. Hogan wrestled for several different companies, including the WWF, over the next few years. In 1983, he returned to the WWF and spent 10 years there. His fame rose quickly.

During his time with the WWF, Hogan developed a good-guy image. In wrestling, good guys are called baby faces. He also showed the world what Hulk Mode could do during his time with the WWF.

Hogan goes into Hulk Mode during a tough match.

In January 1984, Hogan defeated the Iron Sheik for the WWF Championship. Hogan became the most famous wrestler in the United States. Hulkamania, fan excitement for Hogan, spread across the country.

Leati Joseph Anoaʻi, who later became Roman Reigns, was born on May 25, 1985, in Pensacola, Florida. His father, Sika, and his uncle, Afa, competed in the WWF. Their team was the WWF Tag Team Champions in the early 1980s.

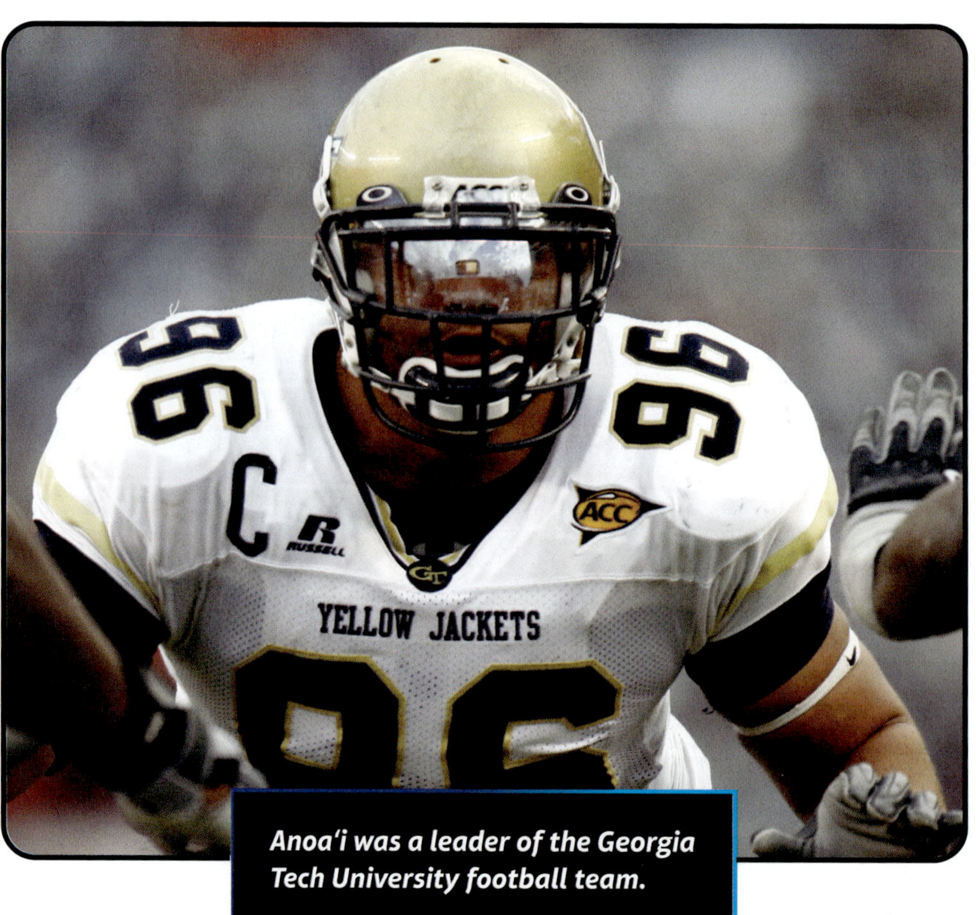

Anoaʻi was a leader of the Georgia Tech University football team.

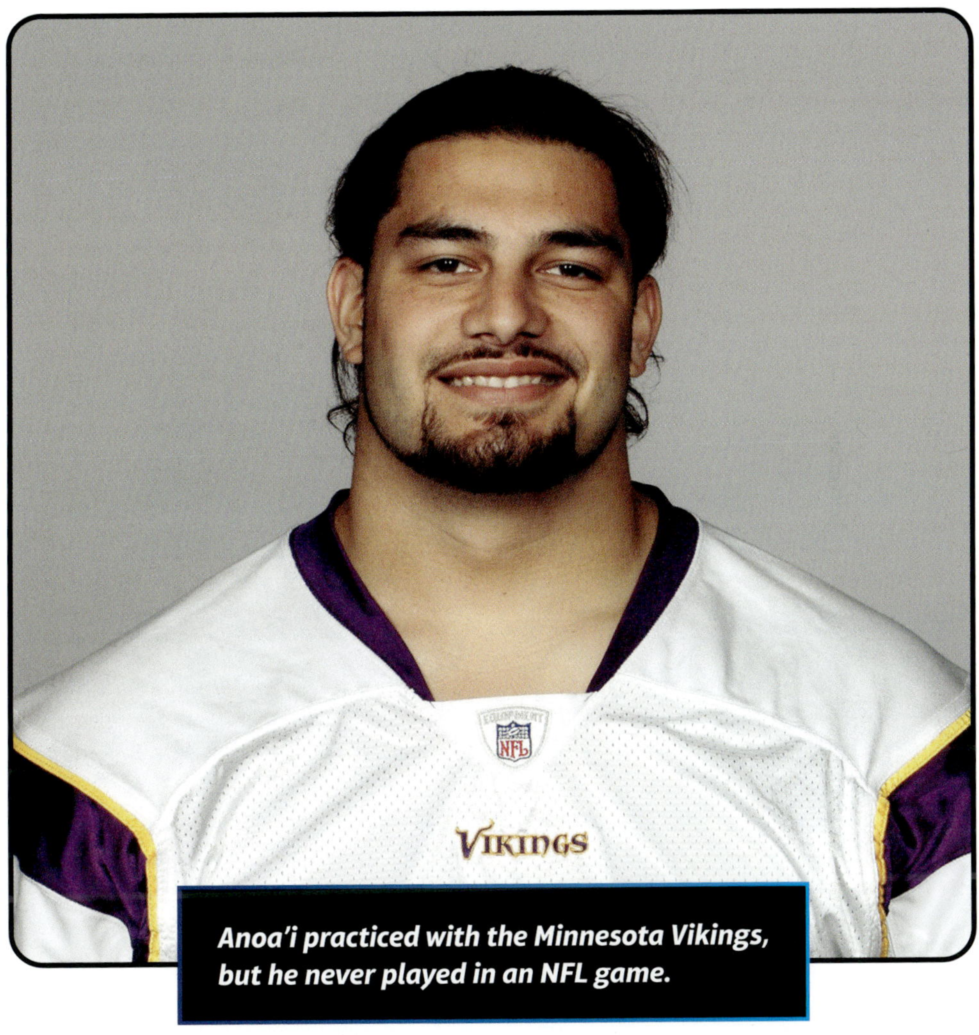

Anoa'i practiced with the Minnesota Vikings, but he never played in an NFL game.

Anoa'i was a star defensive tackle at Georgia Tech University. After college, he joined the Minnesota Vikings of the National Football League. But before he played a game with the Vikings, Anoa'i learned he had cancer. After treatment, he played one season of pro football in the Canadian Football League.

Anoa'i joined the WWE in 2010. At first, he competed as Roman Leakee. He wrestled in the WWE's training company, Florida Championship Wrestling.

Anoa'i dropped the name Roman Leakee in 2012 and began calling himself Roman Reigns in the ring.

In 2012, he made his first WWE television appearance as Roman Reigns at Survivor Series. Reigns was a member of The Shield, a team of wrestling bad guys, or heels. Reigns and teammates Dean Ambrose and Seth Rollins would shake up the WWE for years to come.

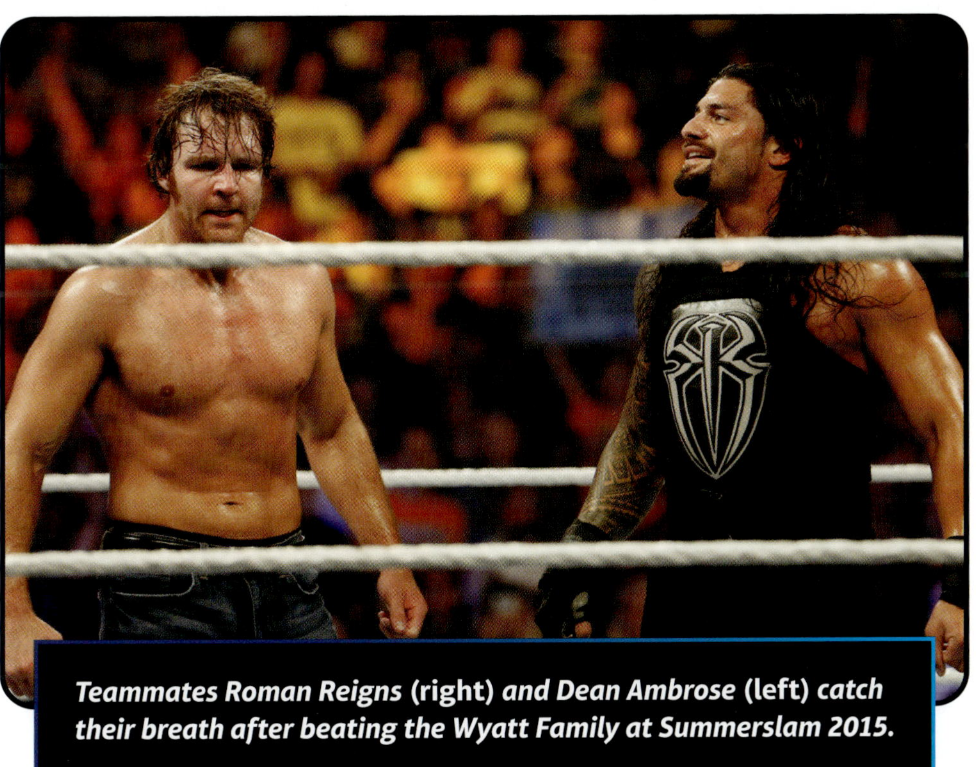

Teammates Roman Reigns (right) and Dean Ambrose (left) catch their breath after beating the Wyatt Family at Summerslam 2015.

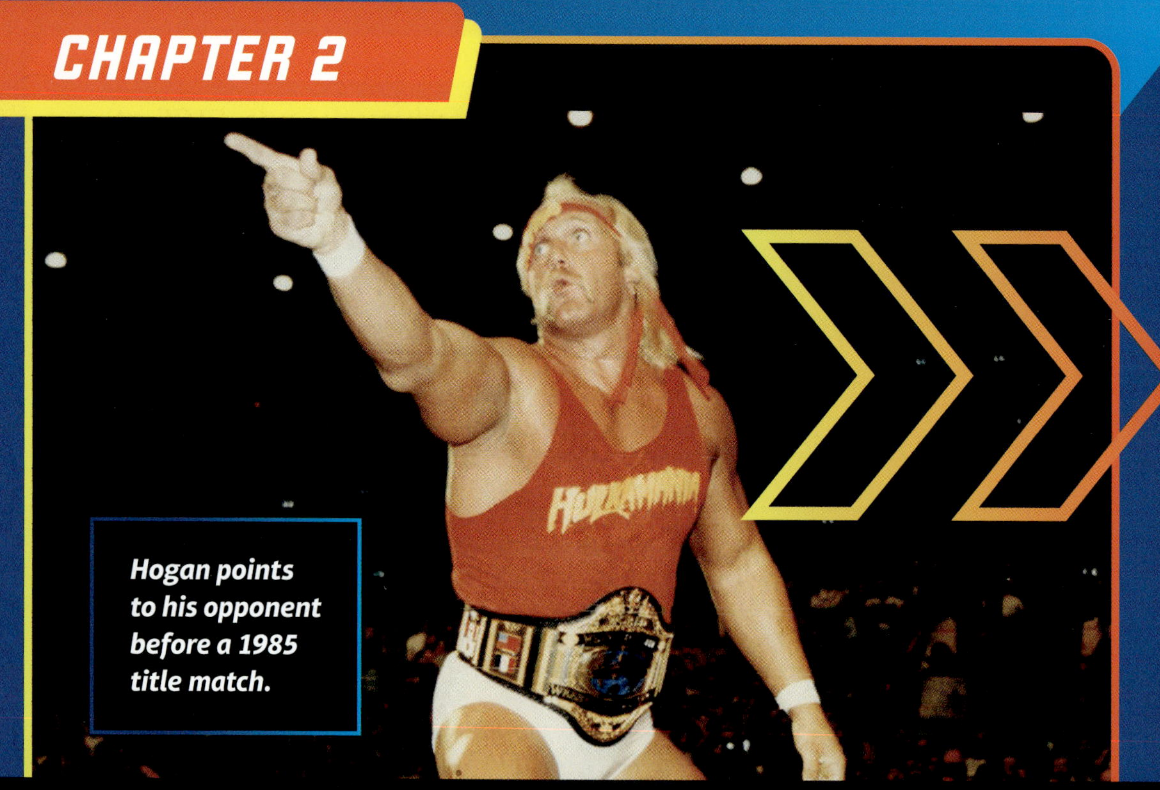

CHAPTER 2

Hogan points to his opponent before a 1985 title match.

GREAT MOMENTS

After winning the WWF title in January 1984, Hogan defended his championship belt against many different heels. One of Hogan's first big feuds as champion was with 6 foot 10 (2.1 m) Big John Studd.

In early 1985, Hogan was the star of the first WrestleMania, a hugely successful event that made wrestling more popular across the US. Hogan's huge muscles, colorful clothes, and high-energy style defined pro wrestling for many fans. He encouraged kids to make good choices and eat healthful foods. Hulkamania T-shirts, hats, and other gear sold around the world. Hogan even appeared on the cover of *Sports Illustrated* magazine in 1985.

Hogan successfully defended his title 471 times between 1984 and 1988. His wins included victories over King Kong Bundy at WrestleMania II and Andre the Giant at

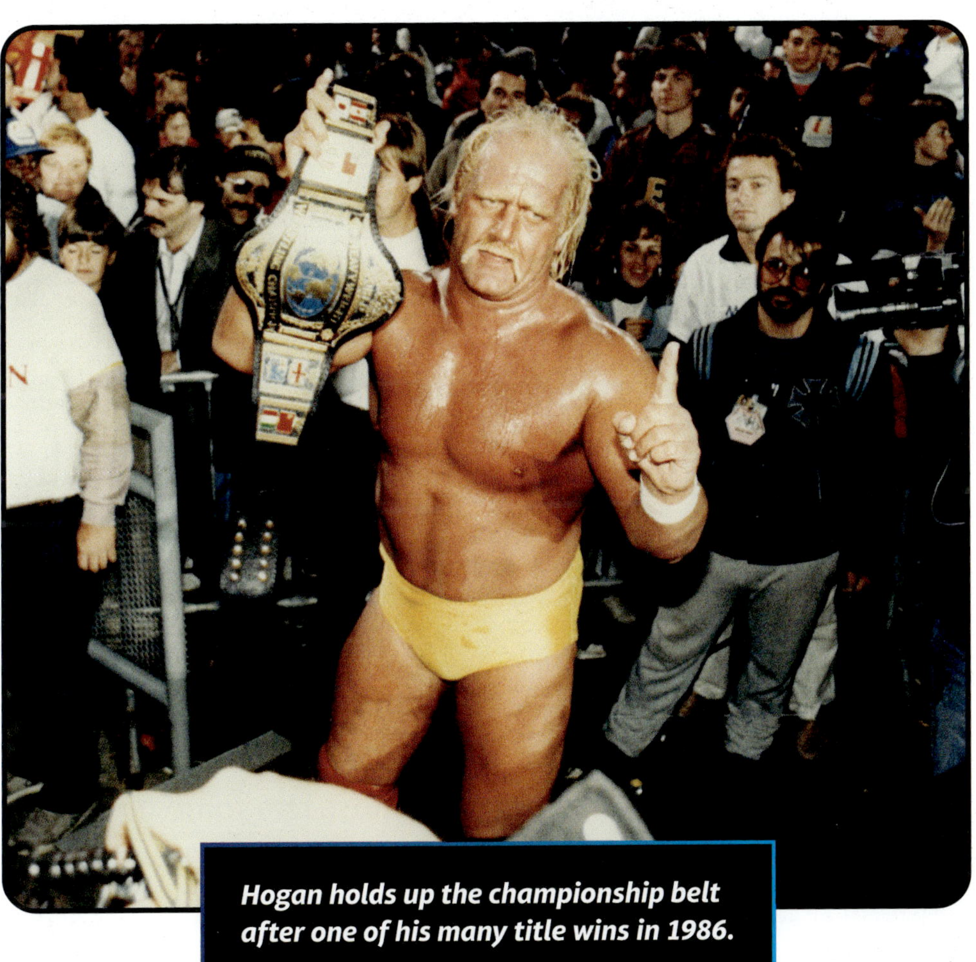

Hogan holds up the championship belt after one of his many title wins in 1986.

Hogan (front) and Ric Flair (back) do battle in a 1994 match in New York.

WrestleMania III. Hogan won the WWE Championship belt four more times in the late 1980s and early 1990s.

In 1994, Hogan left the WWF and joined World Championship Wrestling (WCW). Right away, Hogan won the WCW title from Ric Flair. Hogan held the WCW title six times from 1994 to 1999.

During his time in the WCW, Hogan became a heel. As Hollywood Hulk Hogan, he led a group called the New World Order. The team became one of the most fearsome groups of heels in wrestling history.

Hogan returned to the WWF in 2002. Seventeen years after starring in the first WrestleMania, Hogan lost to Dwayne

"The Rock" Johnson in a classic main event at WrestleMania 18. Hogan won the WWF title for the sixth and final time when he defeated Triple H at WWF Backlash 2002. Hogan was the last title winner before the company became the WWE.

Roman Reigns won the WWE Championship for the first time at Survivor Series 2015. He defeated Dean Ambrose in the final match of a title tournament. Moments later,

Hogan traps The Rock in a headlock during their match at WrestleMania 18.

Sheamus appeared in the arena. He challenged Reigns, and Reigns couldn't refuse. Sheamus won the match, and Reigns would have to wait for another chance at the belt.

Reigns won the title two more times in the coming years. He also earned the WWE's United States Championship and Intercontinental Championship belts.

Although Reigns feuded with many WWE superstars, his matches with Brock Lesnar are among the most memorable. The first two times they fought, Lesnar defeated Reigns, including a classic main event at WrestleMania 34. But at SummerSlam 2018, Reigns's luck changed.

Brock Lesnar lifts Reigns and prepares to slam him to the mat at a 2021 match.

Reigns holds up one of his two title belts in 2022.

Lesnar was about to defeat Reigns by hitting him with a steel chair. But Reigns jumped at Lesnar and landed his signature spear move. Reigns lifted Lesnar's leg and pinned him, taking Lesnar's WWE Universal Championship.

Reigns won the Universal title again in 2020 and has held the belt ever since. He is the longest-running WWE Universal Champion of all time, holding the belt for more than 900 days.

In March 2022, Reigns fought Lesnar again. It was the battle of the Universal Champion and the WWE Champion. The winner of the match would hold both titles. Reigns once again finished the match with a spear move, knocking Lesnar to the mat and pinning him.

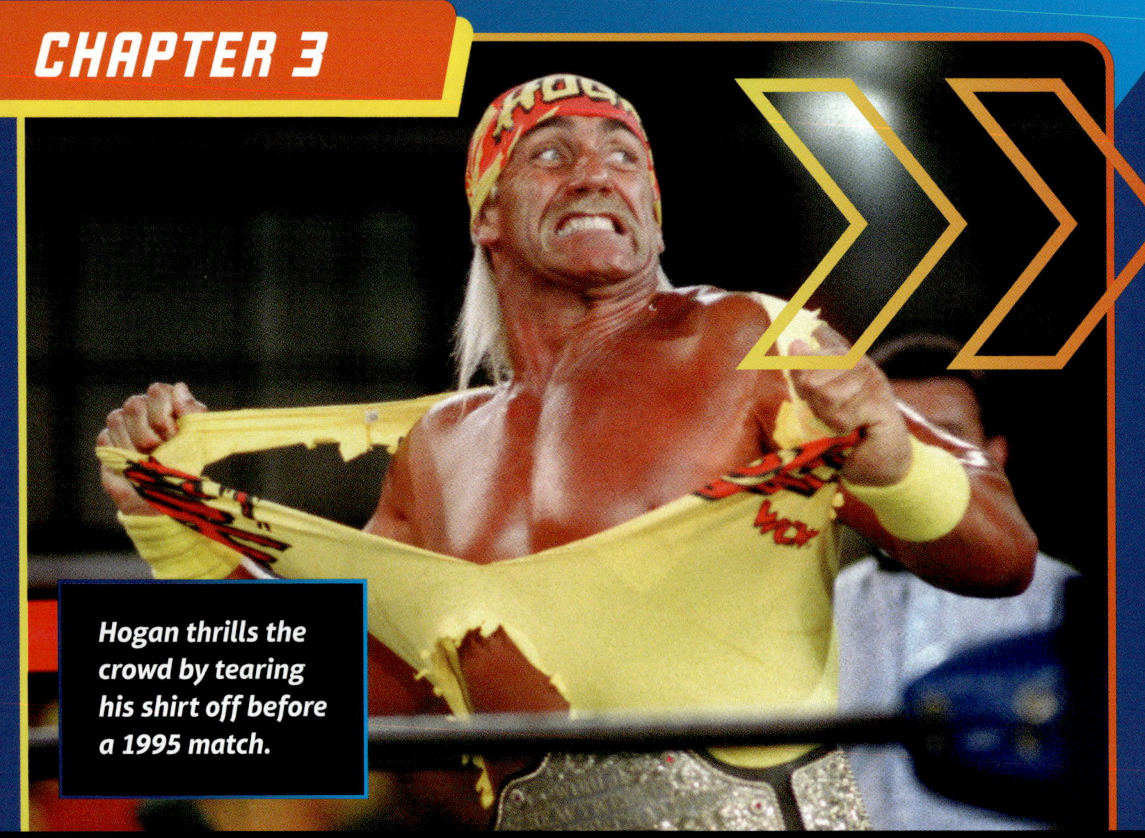

CHAPTER 3

Hogan thrills the crowd by tearing his shirt off before a 1995 match.

CHAMPIONS

Hogan and Reigns are two of the most successful pro wrestlers in the history of the sport. In and out of the ring, they have both been great champions.

Hogan held the WWE Championship six times for a total of 2,185 days. Reigns currently holds the title for the fourth time. By April 2023, he had been champion for more than 480 days.

Hogan held several other titles, including the WCW

Championship six times, and the WWE World Tag
Team Championship once. Reigns holds the WWE
Universal Championship for the second time. He's also
been a WWE Tag Team Champion, US Champion, and
Intercontinental Champion.

   As part of the WWE, Hogan fought in 1,036 one-on-one
matches. He won 853 times, or 82 percent of his matches.
By April 2023, Reigns had fought in 615 one-on-one
matches in the WWE. He won 551 of them, or almost
90 percent.

Reigns (right) defends his titles against Kevin Owens at the 2023 Royal Rumble.

Hogan left the WWE about six years before Reigns joined the company, but they were both pro wrestlers at the same time. Reigns's first pro match was in 2010, and Hogan's last match was in 2012. This dream smackdown could have happened in real life.

Hogan won eight of his 12 WrestleMania matches. Reigns has won six times at WrestleMania, losing only twice. Hogan won the 30-man Royal Rumble event twice, while Reigns won it once.

At the 2023 Royal Rumble, Reigns holds a folding chair in the ring.

Hogan (left) *starred as a pro wrestler named Thunderlips in the film* Rocky III.

Hogan's popularity went beyond the world of pro wrestling. He played a pro wrestler in the movie *Rocky III* and starred in several other movies. Reigns has also found great popularity outside the ring. He appeared in the movie *Fast & Furious Presents: Hobbs & Shaw* and voiced a character on the Disney show *Elena of Avalor*.

In October 2018, Reigns announced that his cancer had returned. He left wrestling for nearly four months to get treatment. He returned to the ring in March 2019.

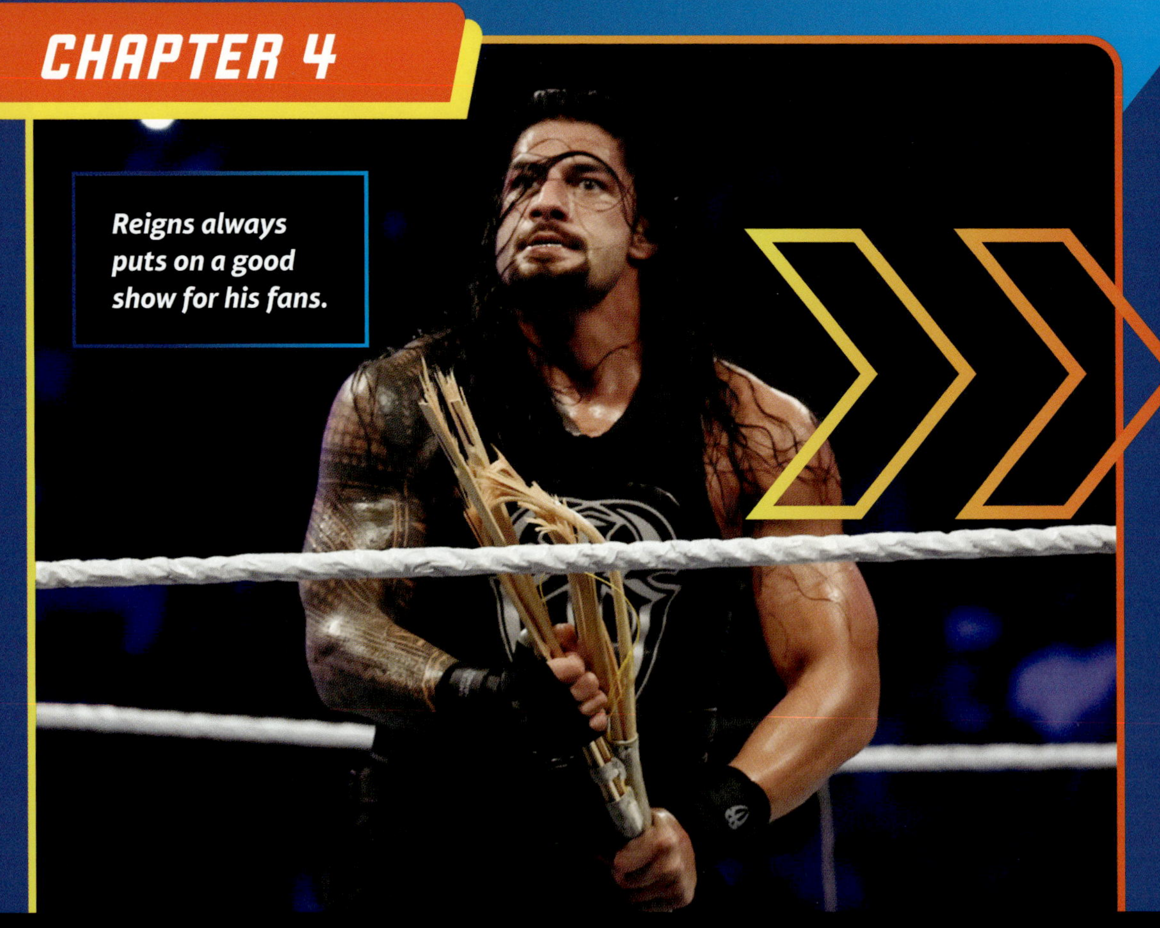

CHAPTER 4

AND THE WINNER IS

Who is the winner of this all-star pro wrestling smackdown? You can decide for yourself. Reigns and Hogan are among the greatest wrestlers of all time, so there is no right or wrong answer. Different people may have different opinions. That's part of the fun of being a sports fan. So who do you think is best? Let's consider their careers.

Hogan holds the advantage in championships, having held the WWE title six times. Reigns has held it four times. But Reigns has also held the WWE Universal title since 2020.

Hogan won 853 times in the WWE compared to Reigns's 551 victories. But Reigns holds the advantage in winning percentage. Hogan won 82 percent of the time, while Reigns has won nearly 90 percent of his matches.

Hogan feuded with some of the greatest legends in pro wrestling history, such as Andre the Giant, Ric Flair, and

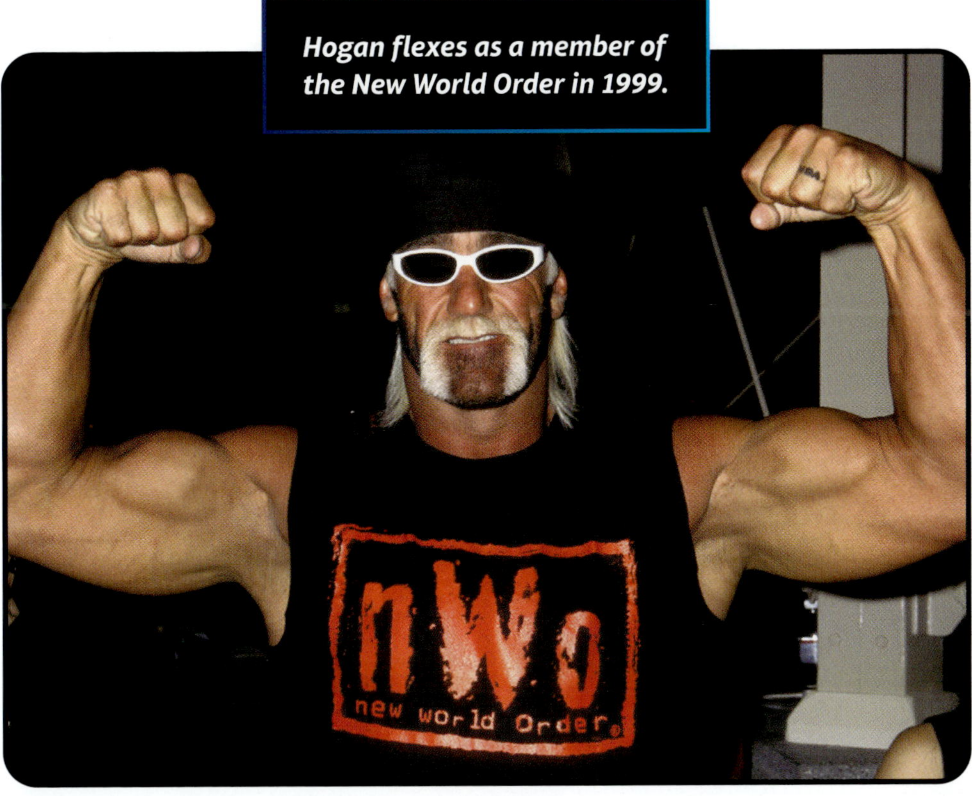

Hogan flexes as a member of the New World Order in 1999.

"Macho Man" Randy Savage. But Reigns has had his own big-time feuds. He has faced off with legends such as John Cena, Braun Stroman, and Brock Lesnar.

Hogan's signature move was the leg drop. Reigns's signature moves are the spear and the Superman punch. The moves can turn a match in his favor.

Both men's careers go beyond the ring. Hogan was a larger-than-life superstar who helped build pro wrestling into the popular sport that it is today. Reigns did great things in the ring even while fighting a deadly disease. In honor of his own fight, he works to help support people battling the same illness.

It's very hard to choose a winner in a smackdown this close. Hogan may be the most well-known pro wrestler of all time. But Reigns has competed while fighting cancer, has stronger signature moves, and continues to rack up wins and championships. We're giving the win to Reigns. Who do you think the winner is? Think it over and make your choice!

"Macho Man" Randy Savage (left) and Hogan (right) teamed up

Reigns holds up two title belts as wrestling fans cheer for their champion.

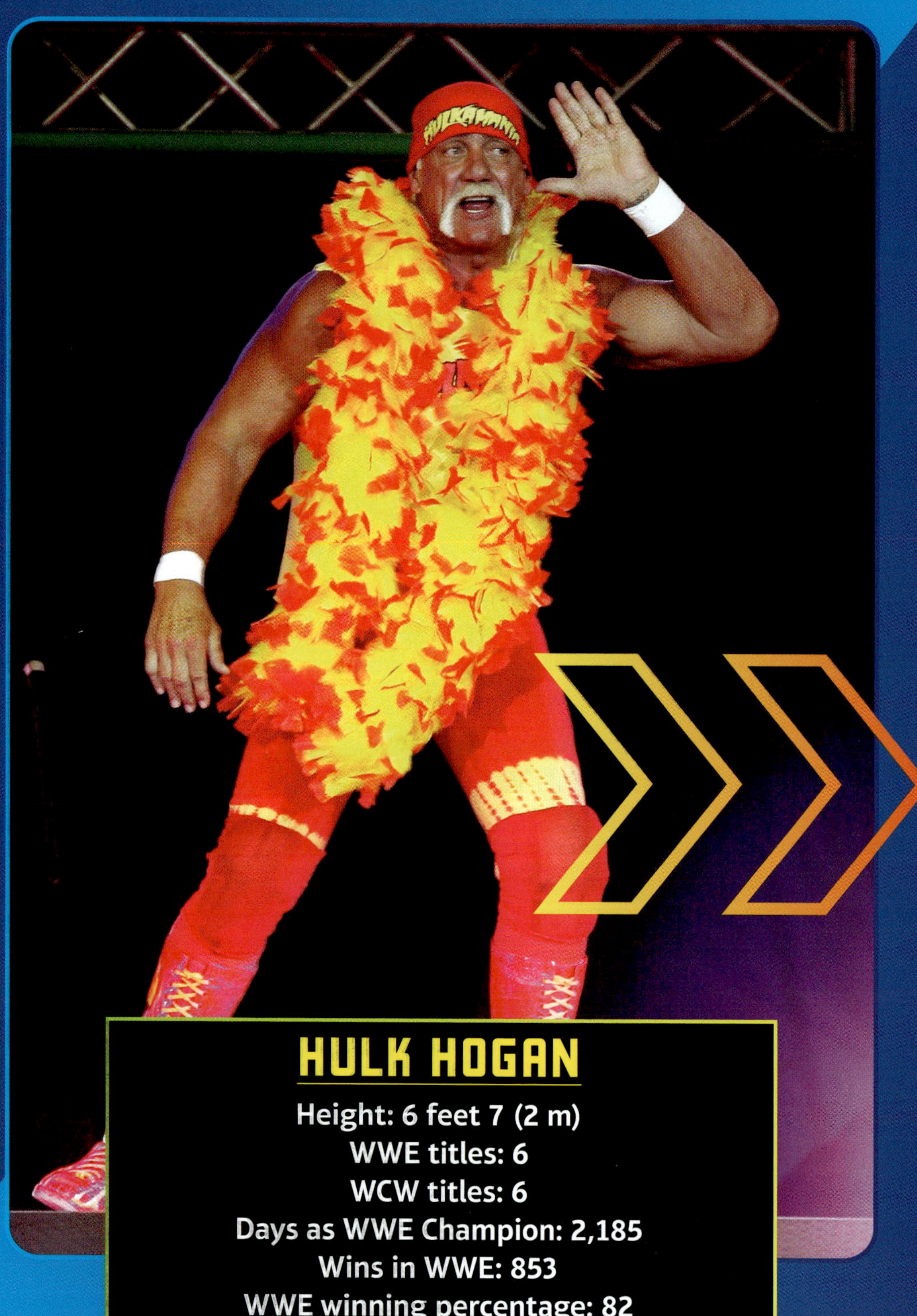

HULK HOGAN

Height: 6 feet 7 (2 m)
WWE titles: 6
WCW titles: 6
Days as WWE Champion: 2,185
Wins in WWE: 853
WWE winning percentage: 82

Stats are accurate through May 2023.

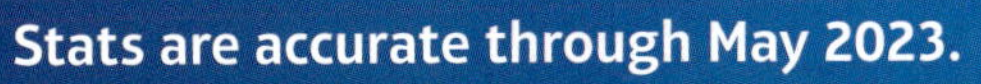

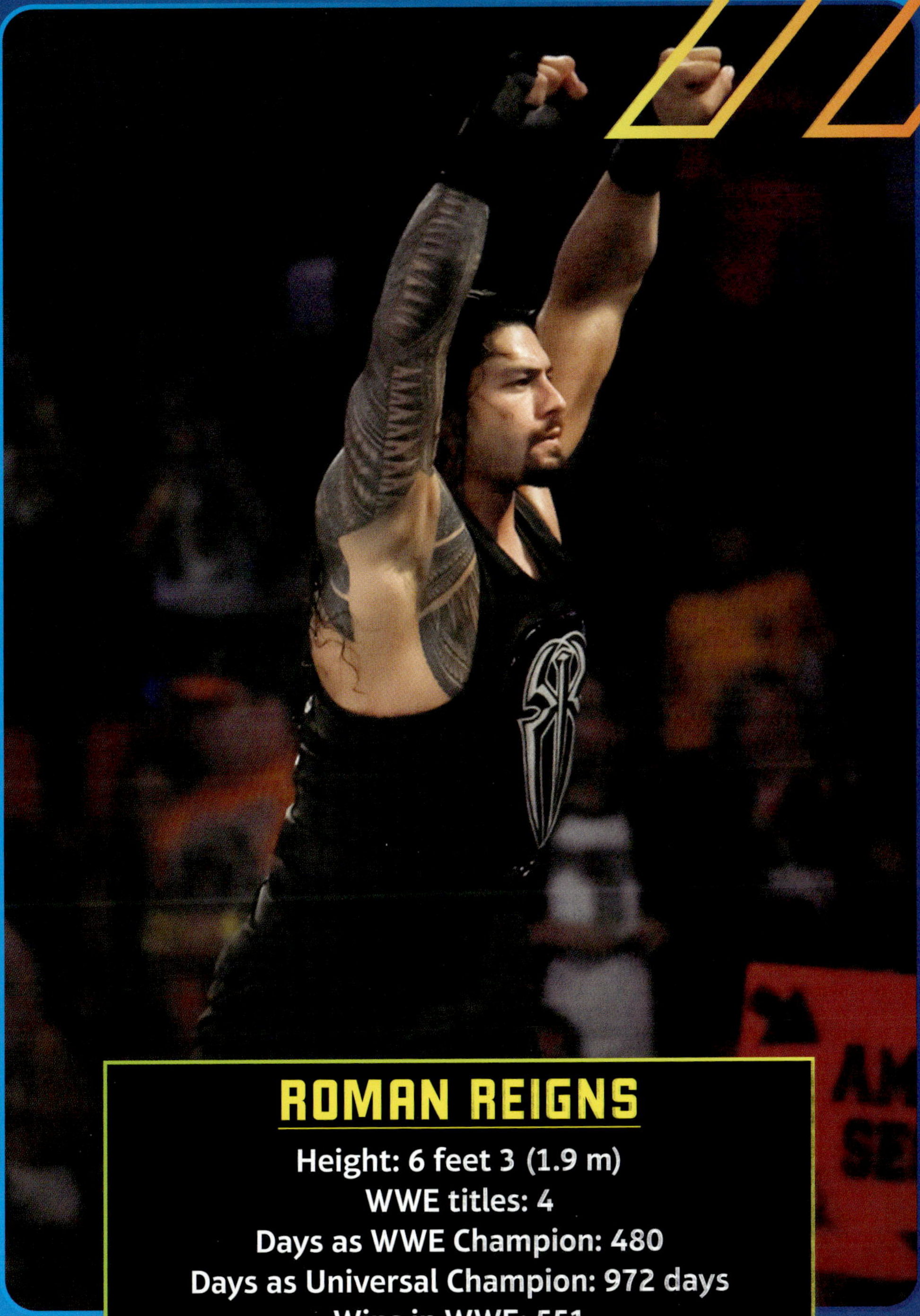

ROMAN REIGNS

Height: 6 feet 3 (1.9 m)
WWE titles: 4
Days as WWE Champion: 480
Days as Universal Champion: 972 days
Wins in WWE: 551
WWE winning percentage: 90

GLOSSARY

baby face: a good-guy wrestler meant to be cheered by fans

body slam: a move where one wrestler picks up another and throws them to the ground

championship belt: a large belt worn by champions in sports such as wrestling and boxing

clothesline: a move where one wrestler attempts to hit an opponent in the neck or chest with an outstretched arm

feud: a long-lasting conflict

heel: a bad-guy wrestler meant to be booed by fans

leg drop: a move where one wrestler drops the back of his leg on top of an opponent's chest or neck

pin: to hold an opponent's shoulders to the ground. Wrestlers can win matches by pinning their opponents.

signature move: a move that a wrestler often uses in important moments

spear: a wrestling move where one wrestler flies through the air and slams his shoulder into his opponent

title: a championship

LEARN MORE

History of WWE Facts for Kids
https://kids.kiddle.co/History_of_WWE

Hulk Hogan Facts for Kids
https://kids.kiddle.co/Hulk_Hogan

Kinley, J. R. *Roman Reigns*. Minnetonka, MN: Kaleidoscope, 2019.

Levit, Joe. *Pro Wrestling's G.O.A.T.* Minneapolis: Lerner Publications, 2022.

Monnig, Alex. *Roman Reigns*. Minneapolis: Abdo, 2023.

WWE Official Site
https://www.wwe.com/

INDEX

Andre the Giant, 5, 15, 25

Florida Championship Wrestling, 12

Georgia Tech University, 11

Hulkamania, 10, 15

Minnesota Vikings, 11

New World Order, 16

Shield, The, 13
spear, 19, 26
Sports Illustrated, 15

World Championship Wrestling (WCW), 16, 20
World Wrestling Entertainment (WWE), 4, 12–13, 16–22, 25
World Wrestling Federation (WWF), 5, 9–10, 14, 16–17

PHOTO ACKNOWLEDGMENTS

Image credits: picture alliance/Contributor/Getty Images, p.4; Yukio Hiraku/AFLO/Newscom, p.5; FAYEZ NURELDINE/Contributor/Getty Images, p.6; Jeffrey Asher/Contributor/Getty Images, p.7; The Stanley Weston Archive/Contributor/Getty Images, p.8; Tony Bock/Contributor/Getty Images, p.9; Rob Tringali/Sportschrome/Contributor/Getty Images, p.10; Getty Images/Stringer/Getty Images, p.11; Ron Elkman/Sports Imagery/Contributor/Getty Images, p.12; JP Yim/Stringer/Getty Images, p.13; Al Dunlop/Contributor/Getty Images, p.14; Tony Bock/Contributor/Getty Images, p.15; Photo By John Barrett/PHOTOlink/Newscom, p.16; George Pimentel/Contributor/Getty Images, p.17; FAYEZ NURELDINE/Contributor/Getty Images, p.18; AMER HILABI/Contributor/Getty Images, p.19; Star Tribune via Getty Images/Contributor/Getty Images, p.20; Alex Bierens de Haan/Stringer/Getty Images, p.21; Alex Bierens de Haan/Stringer/Getty Images, p.22; Michael Ochs Archives/Handout/Getty Images, 23; Ron Elkman/Sports Imagery/Contributor/Getty Images, p.24; Ron Galella/Contributor/Getty Images, p.25; Ron Galella/Contributor/Getty Images, p.26; Alex Bierens de Haan/Stringer/Getty Images, p.27; Paul Kane/Stringer/Getty Images, p.28; Ron Elkman/Sports Imagery/Contributor/Getty Images, p.29

Cover: ullstein bild/Contributor/Getty Images; Luis Santana/ZUMA Press/Newscom